TOP HITS

22 SONGS WITH CHORDS, LYRICS & BASIC TAB

ISBN 978-1-5400-6306-9

HAL•LEONARD®

Visit Hal Leonard Online at
www.halleonard.com

Contact us:
Hal Leonard
7777 West Bluemound Road
Milwaukee, WI 53213
Email: info@halleonard.com

In Europe, contact:
Hal Leonard Europe Limited
42 Wigmore Street
Marylebone, London, W1U 2RN
Email: info@halleonardeurope.com

In Australia, contact:
Hal Leonard Australia Pty. Ltd.
4 Lentara Court
Cheltenham, Victoria, 3192 Australia
Email: info@halleonard.com.au

GUITAR NOTATION LEGEND

Chord Diagrams

CHORD DIAGRAMS graphically represent the guitar fretboard to show correct chord fingerings.

- The letter above the diagram tells the name of the chord.
- The top, bold horizontal line represents the nut of the guitar. Each thin horizontal line represents a fret. Each vertical line represents a string; the low E string is on the far left and the high E string is on the far right.
- A dot shows where to put your fret-hand finger and the number at the bottom of the diagram tells which finger to use.
- The "O" above the string means play it open, while an "X" means don't play the string.

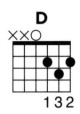

Tablature

TABLATURE graphically represents the guitar fingerboard. Each horizontal line represents a string, and each number represents a fret.

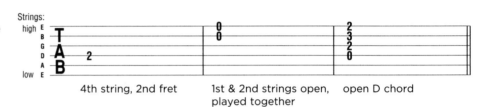

4th string, 2nd fret · 1st & 2nd strings open, played together · open D chord

Definitions for Special Guitar Notation

HAMMER-ON: Strike the first (lower) note with one finger, then sound the higher note (on the same string) with another finger by fretting it without picking.

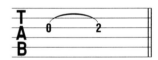

PULL-OFF: Place both fingers on the notes to be sounded. Strike the first note and without picking, pull the finger off to sound the second (lower) note.

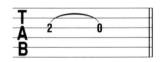

LEGATO SLIDE: Strike the first note and then slide the same fret-hand finger up or down to the second note. The second note is not struck.

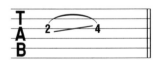

SHIFT SLIDE: Same as legato slide, except the second note is struck.

Additional Musical Definitions

N.C. · No chord. Instrument is silent.

 · Repeat measures between signs.

All About That Bass

Words and Music by Kevin Kadish and Meghan Trainor

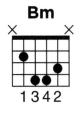
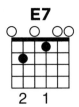

CHORUS 1

Moderately fast

N.C.   A
Because you know I'm all about that bass, 'bout that bass. No treble.

   Bm
I'm all about that bass, 'bout that bass. No treble.

   E7
I'm all about that bass, 'bout that bass. No treble.

   A
I'm all about that bass, 'bout that bass, bass, bass, bass.

VERSE 1

   A
   Yeah, it's pretty clear, I ain't no size two.

Bm
   But I can shake it, shake it like I'm supposed to do.

E7
   'Cause I got that boom, boom that all the boys chase

       A
And all   the right junk in all the right places.

VERSE 2

   A
   I see the magazine workin' that Photoshop.

Bm
   We know that stuff ain't real. C'mon now, make it stop.

E7
   If you got beauty, beauty just raise 'em up

      N.C.(A)
'Cause ev'ry inch of you is perfect from the bottom to the top.

VERSE 3

         A   **Bm**
Yeah, my mama she told me don't worry about your size.

       E7   **A**
She says, "Boys like a little more booty to hold at night."

                                                Bm
You know I won't be no stick figure, silicone Barbie doll.

      E7   **A**
So, if that's what you're into then go ahead and move along.

CHORUS 2

N.C.   **A**
Because you know I'm all about that bass, 'bout that bass. No treble.

    Bm
I'm all about that bass, 'bout that bass. No treble.

    E7
I'm all about that bass, 'bout that bass. No treble.

    A
I'm all about that bass, 'bout that bass, hey.

VERSE 4

       A
I'm bringing booty back.

                         Bm
Go ahead and tell them skinny bitches that.

                          E7
Nah, I'm just playin'. I know you think you're fat. But I'm here to tell ya ev'ry

N.C.(A)
inch of you is perfect from the bottom to the top.

REPEAT VERSE 3

CHORUS 3 (PLAY 3 TIMES)

N.C.   **A**
Because you know I'm all about that bass, 'bout that bass. No treble.

    Bm
I'm all about that bass, 'bout that bass. No treble.

    E7
I'm all about that bass, 'bout that bass. No treble.

    A
I'm all about that bass, 'bout that bass.

OUTRO

| A | | | Bm | | | |
| E7 | | | A | | | |

All of Me

Words and Music by John Stephens and Toby Gad

(Capo 1st Fret)

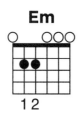 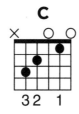

Em   C   G   D   Am

1 2   3 2 1   3 2   4   1 3 2   2 3 1

INTRO

Moderately

| Em | C | G | D | ‖

VERSE 1

```
    Em            C                      G               D                Em
     What would I do without your smart mouth drawin' me in and you kicking me out?
              C        G          D        Em
    You've got my head spinnin', no kiddin'. I can't pin you down.
            C              G               D             Em
    What's goin' on in that beautiful mind?   I'm on your magical mystery ride,
           C        G                  D        Am
    and I'm so dizzy, don't know what hit me but I'll be al - right.
```

PRE-CHORUS

```
      Am              G         D         Am
    My head's under - water, but I'm breathin' fine.
                        G         D
    You're crazy and I'm out of my mind.
```

CHORUS 1

```
      G          Em
    'Cause all of me loves all of you.
            C                                    D
    Love your curves and all your edges, all your perfect imperfections.
          G              Em
    Give your all to me, I'll give my all to you.
            C                          D
    You're my end and my beginning. Even when I lose, I'm winning.
                    Em    C    G    D
    'Cause I give you all      of me,
                    Em    C    G    D
    and you give me all      of you,    oh.
```

VERSE 2

```
Em              C                    G                    D                      Em
    How many times do I have to tell you, even when you're crying you're beautiful too.
```

```
                 C        G        D              Em
    The world is beating you down; I'm around through every mood.
```

```
                 C              G                  D                  Em
    You're my downfall, you're my muse, my worst distraction, my rhythm and blues.
```

```
                 C        G        D        Am
    I can't stop singin', it's ringin' in my   head for you.
```

REPEAT PRE-CHORUS

REPEAT CHORUS 1

BRIDGE

```
                 Am             G        D        Am
    Give me all of you.  Cards on the table, we're both showing hearts.
```

```
             G              D
    Risking it all, though it's hard.
```

CHORUS 2

```
             G              Em
    'Cause all of me loves all of you.
```

```
                 C                              D
    Love your curves and all your edges, all your perfect imperfections.
```

```
             G              Em
    Give your all to me, I'll give my all to you.
```

```
             C                          D
    You're my end and my beginning. Even when I lose, I'm winning.
```

```
                 Em      C        G        D
    'Cause I give you all         of me,
```

```
                 Em      C        G        D
    and you give me all         of you.
```

```
             Em      C        G        D
    I give you all         of me,
```

```
                 Em      C        G        D
    and you give me all         of you,      oh.
```

Chasing Cars

Words and Music by Gary Lightbody, Tom Simpson,
Paul Wilson, Jonathan Quinn and Nathan Connolly

A
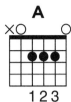
1 2 3

E/G♯

3 1 4

Dsus2

1 3

VERSE 1

Moderately

A   E/G♯   Dsus2   A
We'll do it all,   ev'rything   on our own.

       E/G♯   Dsus2   A
We don't need   anything   or anyone.

CHORUS

   A   E/G♯
If I lay here, if I just lay here,

   Dsus2   A
Would you lie with me and just forget the world?

VERSE 2

   A   E/G♯   Dsus2   A
I don't quite know   how to say   how I feel.

       E/G♯   Dsus2   A
Those three words,   I said too much,   then not enough.

REPEAT CHORUS

VERSE 3

                      A   **E/G♯**
Forget what we're told before we get too old.

           Dsus2   **A**
Show me a garden that's bursting into life.

                  E/G♯   **Dsus2**   **A**
Let's waste time   chasing cars   around our heads.

REPEAT CHORUS

VERSE 4

             A   **E/G♯**
All that I am, all that I ever was

            Dsus2   **A**
is here in your perfect eyes, they're all I can see.

                             E/G♯
I don't know where, confused about how as well.

           Dsus2   **A**
Just know that these things will never change for us at all.

REPEAT CHORUS

City of Stars

from LA LA LAND

Music by Justin Hurwitz
Lyrics by Benj Pasek & Justin Paul

(Capo 3rd Fret)

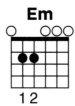
Em

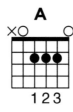
A

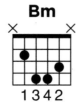
Bm

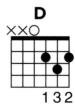
D

Dmaj7

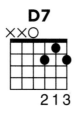
D7

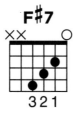
F#7

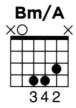
Bm/A

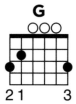
G

INTRO

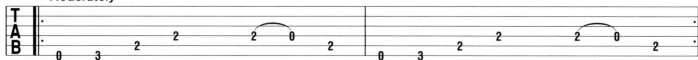

Moderately

VERSE 1

Em   **A**   **Bm**
City of stars,   are you shining just for me?

Em   **A**   **D**
City of stars,   there's so much that I can't see.

Em **A**   **D**   **Dmaj7**   **D7**
Who knows?   I felt it from the first embrace I shared with you

Em   **F#7**   **Bm**   **Bm/A**
that now our dreams may fin'lly come true.

VERSE 2

Em   A   Bm
City of stars,   just one thing ev'rybody wants,

Em   A   D   Dmaj7
there in the bars   and through the smoke screen of the crowded restaurants;

     Em   A   D   Dmaj7   D7
it's love.   Yes, all we're looking for is love from someone else.

    Em   F#7
A rush, a glance, a touch, a dance.

BRIDGE

    G   A   F#7
A look in somebody's eyes to light up the skies,

           Bm
to open the world and send it reeling.

    G   A   Bm
A voice that says, "I'll be here, and you'll be alright."

G   A   F#7
I don't care if I know just where I will go,

           Bm   G   F#7
'cause all that I need's this crazy feeling, a rat - tat - tat on my heart...

         Bm   Bm/A
Think I want it to stay.

OUTRO

Em   A   D
City of stars,   are you shining just for me?

Em   F#7   Bm
City of stars,   you never shined so brightly.

Counting Stars

Words and Music by Ryan Tedder

(Capo 4th Fret)

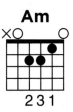 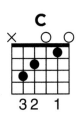 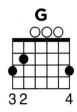  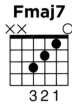 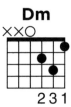

CHORUS

Moderately slow

Am   C   G   Fmaj7

Lately I been, I been losing sleep   dreamin' about the things that we could be. But

Am   C   G   Fmaj7

baby, I been, I been prayin' hard.   Said no more countin' dollars, we'll be countin' stars.

(First Chorus Only)

                                   N.C.

Yeah, we'll be countin'   stars.

INTERLUDE

Moderately

‖: Am | C | G | F   :‖

VERSE 1

                Am   C

I see this life like a swingin' vine, swing my heart across the line.

G   Fmaj7

In my face is flashin' signs,   seek it out and ye shall find.

Am   C

Old, but I'm not that old. Young, but I'm not that bold. And

G   Fmaj7

I don't think the world is sold   on just doin' what we're told.

PRE-CHORUS 1

Am   C   G   F

    I feel something so right doin' the wrong thing.

Am   C   G   F

    And I feel something so wrong when doin' the right thing.

                                   N.C.

I couldn't lie, couldn't lie, couldn't lie. Everything that kills me makes me feel alive.

REPEAT CHORUS (2 TIMES)

REPEAT INTERLUDE (NO REPEAT)

VERSE 2

```
            Am                      C
I feel your love, and I feel it burn down this river, every turn.

G                      Fmaj7
Hope is a four-letter word.  Make that money, watch it burn.

Am                      C
Old, but I'm not that old. Young, but I'm not that bold.  And

G                      Fmaj7
I don't think the world is sold     on just doin' what we're told.
```

PRE-CHORUS 2

```
Am          C              G              F
      And I    feel something so wrong when doin' the right thing.

                                  N.C.
I couldn't lie, couldn't lie, couldn't lie.  Everything that downs me makes me wanna fly.
```

REPEAT CHORUS (2 TIMES)

BRIDGE

Play 4 times

```
||: N.C. (Am)                    |                              :||
     Take  that  money,  watch  it  burn.  Sink  in the river the lessons I've learned.

F                Dm
Everything that  kills me…  makes me feel alive.
```

REPEAT CHORUS (2 TIMES)

OUTRO

```
Am                      C
Take that money, watch it burn.  Sink in the river the lessons I've learned.

G                      F
Take that money, watch it burn.  Sink in the river the lessons I've learned.

Am                      C
Take that money, watch it burn.  Sink in the river the lessons I've learned.

G                      N.C.
Take that money, watch it burn.  Sink in the river the lessons I've learned.
```

Despacito

Words and Music by Luis Fonsi, Erika Ender, Justin Bieber,
Jason Boyd, Marty James Garton and Ramon Ayala

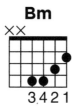
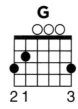
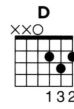
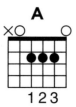

VERSE 1

Bm
C'mon on over in my direction.   G So thankful for that, it's such a blessin', yeah.   D

A
Turn every situation into heaven, yeah. Oh, oh. Bm You are my sunrise on the darkest day.   G

D
Got me feelin' some kind of way. Make me wanna savor every moment slowly, slowly. A

Bm
You fit me tailor-made love, how you put it on.   G Got the only key, know how to turn it on.

D
The way you nibble on my ear, the only words I wanna hear: A Baby, take it slow so we can last long.

VERSE 2

Bm
Tú, tú eres el imán y yo soy el metal. G Me voy acercando y voy armando el plan. D

A
Sólo con pensarlo se acelera el pulso. Oh, yeah. Bm Ya, ya me está gustando más de lo normal. G

D
Todos mis sentidos vanpidiendo más. A Esto hay que tomarlo sin ningún a puro.

CHORUS 1

N.C. Bm
Despcito. Quiero respirar tu cuello despacito. G Deja que te diga cosas al oído, para que te D

A N.C. Bm
acuerdes si no estás conmigo. Despacito. Quiero desnudarte a besos despacito, firmo en G

D
las paredes de tu laberinto, y hacer de tu cuerpo todo un manuscripto. A

VERSE 3

Bm
Quiero ver bailar tu pelo, quiero ser tu ritmo, G que le enseñes a mi boca, D tus lugares favoritos. A

Bm
Déjame sobrepasar tus zonas de peligro, G hasta provocar tus gritos, D y que olvides tu apellido. A

VERSE 4

N.C.   Bm   G

Si te pido un beso, ven dámelo. Yo sé que estás pensándolo. Llevo tiempo intentándolo,

                                          D

mami esto es dando y dándolo. Sabes que tu corazón conmigo te hace bang bang.

                   A   N.C.   Bm

Sabes que esa beba está buscando de mi bang bang. Ven prueba de mi boca para ver como te sabe.

                   G   D

Quiero, quiero, quiero ver quánto amor a ti te cabe. Yo no tengo prisa, yo me quiero dar el viaje,

                   A   N.C.

empecemos lento, después salvaje. Pasito a pa -

VERSE 5

Bm   G   D

sito, suave suave cito. Nos vamos pegando poquito a paquito cuando tú me besas

                            A   N.C.   Bm

con esa de streza, veo que eres malicia con delicadeza. Pasito a pasito, suave suavecito.

                 G   D

No vamos pegando poquito a poquito. Y es que esa belleza en un rompeca bezas,

                 A   N.C.

pero pa' montarlo aquí tengo la pieza. ¡O ye!

REPEAT CHORUS 1

REPEAT VERSE 3

CHORUS 2

N.C.   Bm   G

Despacito. This is how we do it down in Puerto Rico. I just wanna hear you screaming

                   D   A

"¡Ay Bendito!" I can move forever se queda contigo. Pasito a pa -

VERSE 6

Bm   G

sito, suave suavecito. Nos vamos pegando poquito a poquito a poquito.

                                            (Que le enseñes a mi

D   A   Bm

                                 Pasito pasito, suave suavecito.

boca, tus lugares favoritos.)

                 G   D   A

Nos vamos pegando, poquito a poquito.   Y que olvides tu apellido.

                       (Hasta provocar tus gritos.)

N.C.

Despacito.

Fix You

Words and Music by Guy Berryman, Jon Buckland, Will Champion and Chris Martin

(Capo 3rd Fret)

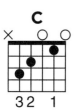 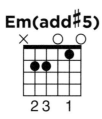 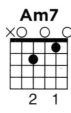 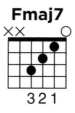 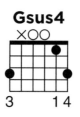 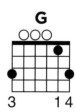

VERSE 1

Slowly

        C   Em(add♯5)   Am7   Em(add♯5)
When you try your best but you don't succeed.

        C   Em(add♯5)   Am7   Em(add♯5)
When you get what you want but not what you need.

        C   Em(add♯5)   Am7   Em(add♯5)
When you feel so tired but you can't sleep.

        C   Em(add♯5)   Am7   Em(add♯5)
Stuck in reverse.

VERSE 2

        C   Em(add♯5)   Am7   Em(add♯5)
And the tears coming streaming down your face

        C   Em(add♯5)   Am7   Em(add♯5)
when you lose something you can't replace.

        C   Em(add♯5)   Am7   Em(add♯5)
When you love someone but it goes to waste

        C   Em(add♯5)   Am7   Em(add♯5)
could it be worse?

CHORUS 1

Fmaj7   C Gsus4 G   Fmaj7   C Gsus4   G
Lights will guide   you home, and ig - nite   your

Fmaj7   C Gsus4 G   C   Em(add♯5)   Am7   Em(add♯5)
bones.   And I will try   to fix you.

VERSE 3

```
          C           Em(add♯5)      Am7           Em(add♯5)
And  high  up  above  or  down  below

            C           Em(add♯5)      Am7           Em(add♯5)
when  you're  too  in  love  to  let  it  go.

          C           Em(add♯5)      Am7           Em(add♯5)
But  if  you  never  try  you'll  never  know

              C           Em(add♯5)      Am7           Em(add♯5)
just  what  you're  worth.
```

CHORUS 2

```
Fmaj7              C  Gsus4  G     Fmaj7      C  Gsus4   G
         Lights will guide      you home, and ig - nite         your

Fmaj7              C  Gsus4   G
bones.      And  I  will  try       to  fix  you.
```

INTERLUDE

```
‖: C              |Fmaj7            |C              |Gsus4  G              |

   Am7            |Fmaj7            |C              |Gsus4  G            :‖
```

BRIDGE

```
C                F              C                      Gsus4        G
   Tears  stream   down  your  face,    when  you  lose  something  you  cannot  replace.

Am7              F                    C      Gsus4        G
   Tears  stream   down  your  face  and  I....

C                F              C                      Gsus4            G
   Tears  stream   down  your  face,    I  promise  you  I  will  learn  from  my  mistakes.

Am7              F                    C        Gsus4          G
   Tears  stream   down  your  face  and  I....
```

CHORUS 3

```
Fmaj7              C  Gsus4  G     Fmaj7      C  Gsus4   G
         Lights will guide      you home, and ig - nite         your

Fmaj7              C  Gsus4  G          C
bones.      And  I  will  try       to  fix  you.
```

Jar of Hearts

Words and Music by Barrett Yeretsian, Christina Perri and Drew Lawrence

(Capo 3rd Fret)

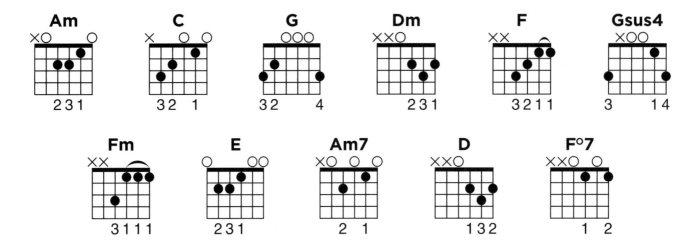

VERSE 1

Moderately slow

```
Am                              C                    G                           Dm
    I know I can't take one more   step towards you,   'cause all that's waiting is regret.
Am                              C                    G                           F
    And don't you know I'm not your   ghost anymore,   you lost the love I loved the most.
```

PRE-CHORUS

```
Dm                F   Am  G  Dm              F              Gsus4      G
    I learned to live half alive,   and now you want me one more     time.
```

CHORUS 1

```
C                              G                Am  ·
    And who do you think you are, running 'round leaving scars,
                    F       Fm          C
collecting your jar of hearts and tearing love apart?
                    G        ·                Am
You're gonna catch a cold from the ice inside your soul.
                    F       Fm          C
So don't come back for me. Who do you think you are?
```

VERSE 2

```
Am                            C      G                      Dm
   I  hear  you're  asking  all  around    if  I  am  anywhere  to  be     found.
Am                            C      G                          F
   But  I  have  grown  too  strong     to  ever  fall  back  in  your  arms.
```

REPEAT PRE-CHORUS

REPEAT CHORUS

BRIDGE

```
     Am          E          Am7    D      Am              E          Am7        D
   And  it  took  so  long  just  to  feel  alright,  remember  how  to  put  back  the  light  in  my  eyes.
     Am          E          Am7          D          Am          E        Am7    D
   I  wish  I  had  missed  the  first  time  that  we  kissed  'cause  you  broke  all  your  promises.
        F                              E
   And  now  you're  back,  you  don't  get  to  get  me  back.
```

CHORUS 2 (2 TIMES)

```
   C                          G                      Am
     And  who  do  you  think  you  are,  running  'round  leaving  scars,
              F      Fm          C
   collecting  your  jar  of  hearts  and  tearing  love  apart?
              G                          Am
   You're  gonna  catch  a  cold  from  the  ice  inside  your  soul.
              F      Fm                  C
   So  don't  come  back  for  me.   Don't  come  back  at  all.
```

OUTRO

```
F°7                C
Who  do  you  think  you  are?
F°7                C
Who  do  you  think  you  are?
F°7                C
Who  do  you  think  you  are?
```

Let It Go

Words and Music by James Bay and Paul Barry

(Capo 1st Fret)

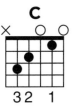 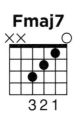 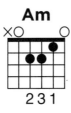 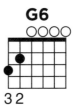 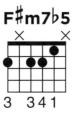 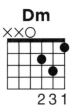

INTRO

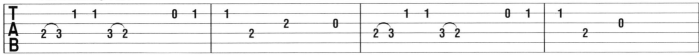

Moderately fast

VERSE 1

```
C                   Fmaj7                    Am   G6   C            Fmaj7
From walking home       and talking loads,                seeing shows
```

```
                   Am   G6   C            Fmaj7              Am   G6
in evening clothes with you.      From nervous touch      and getting drunk
```

```
C          Fmaj7                        Am   G6
to staying up       and waking up with you.
```

PRE-CHORUS 1

```
       Am                  C                        F♯m7♭5      Fmaj7
But now we're sleeping at the edge,  holding something we don't need.
```

```
       Am              C                  F♯m7♭5
All this delusion in our heads    is gonna bring us to our knees.
```

CHORUS 1

```
       Fmaj7 C       Am  G6                 Dm  C         G6
So come on, let it go.    Just let it be.  Why don't you be you    and I'll be me?
```

```
         Fmaj7 C          Am   G6                   Dm  C       G6
Everything that's broke    leave it to the breeze.  Why don't you be you   and I'll be me,
```

and I'll be me?

REPEAT INTRO

VERSE 2

```
    C                    Fmaj7              Am  G6  C              Fmaj7
From throwing clothes     across the floor        to teeth and claws

                        Am   G6        Fmaj7              Am    G6
and slamming doors at you.      If this is all     we're living for

            C             Fmaj7          Am    G6
why are we doing it, doing it, doing it anymore?
```

PRE-CHORUS 2

```
        Am              C                         F#m7♭5      Fmaj7
I used to recognize myself;   it's funny how reflections change.

        Am                      C                    F#m7♭5
When we're becoming something else,   I think it's time to walk away.
```

REPEAT CHORUS 1

REPEAT INTRO

BRIDGE

```
Dm                              C
  Try to fit your hand inside of mine when we know it just don't belong.

G6                                      Am
  There's no force on earth could make it feel right, no. Whoa.

Dm                              C
  Try to push this problem up the hill when it's just too heavy to hold.

G6                        Am
  Think now's the time to let it slide.
```

CHORUS 2

```
              Fmaj7 C      Am   G6            Dm   C       G6
So, come on, let it go.     Just let it be.   Why don't you be you     and I'll be me?

              Fmaj7  C      Am   G6           Dm   C         G6
Everything that's broke,     leave it to the breeze.   Let the ashes fall,     forget about me.

              Fmaj7 C      Am  G6            Dm  C       G6
Come on, let it go.     Just let it be.   Why don't you be you     and I'll be me,

and I'll be me?
```

OUTRO

Love Story

Words and Music by Taylor Swift

(Capo 2nd Fret)

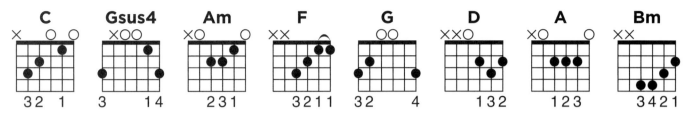

INTRO

Moderately

VERSE 1

C   F
We were both young when I first saw you. I close my eyes and the flashback starts. I'm

Am   F   C
standing there on a balcony in summer air. See the lights, see the party, the ball gowns.

F   Am   Gsus4   G
See you make your way through the crowd and say hello. Little did I   know   that

PRE-CHORUS 1

F   Gsus4   Am
you were Romeo. You were throwing pebbles and my daddy said, "Stay away from

C   F   Gsus4   Am F Gsus4
Juliet." And I was crying on the staircase, begging you, "Please don't go."   And I said,

CHORUS 1

C   Gsus4
"Romeo, take me somewhere we can be alone. I'll be waiting; all there's left to do is run.

Am   F   G
You'll be the prince and I'll be the princess. It's a love story. Baby, just say yes."

INTERLUDE

So

VERSE 2

C   F
I sneak out to the garden to see you. We keep quiet 'cause we're dead if they knew.

                     Am   Gsus4   G
So close your eyes, escape this town for a little while.   Oh, oh , 'cause

PRE-CHORUS 2

F   Gsus4   Am
you were Romeo, I was a scarlet letter and my daddy said, "Stay away from

C   F   Gsus4   Am F Gsus4
Juliet." But you were everything to me. I was beggin' you "Please don't go."   And I said,

REPEAT CHORUS 1

CHORUS 2 *(Play 2 times)*

2nd time, guitar solo

C   Gsus4
Romeo, save me. They're try'n' to tell me how to feel. This love is difficult, but it's, uh, real.

Am   F   G
Don't be afraid, we'll make it out of this mess. It's a love story. Baby, just say yes.

BRIDGE

                  Am   F   C   Gsus4
I got tired of waiting,   wondering if you were ever coming around.

                        Am   F   C   G
My faith i n you was   fading when I met you on the outskirts of town. And I said,

CHORUS 3

C   Gsus4
"Romeo, save me. I've been feeling so alone. I keep waiting for you, but you never come."

   Am   F   Gsus4   N.C.
Is this in my head? I don't know what to think. He knelt to the ground and pulled out a ring and said,

CHORUS 4

D   A
"Marry me, Juliet. You'll never have to be alone. I love you and that's all I really know.

Bm   G   A
I talked to your dad, go pick out a white dress. It's a love story. Baby, just say

OUTRO

D   A   Bm   G   D
    yes." Oh, oh, oh.   Oh, oh, oh,   oh. 'Cause we were both young when I first saw you.

Love Yourself

Words and Music by Justin Bieber, Benjamin Levin,
Ed Sheeran, Joshua Gudwin and Scott Braun

(Capo 4th Fret)

C	G/B	Am	Dm	F	Fsus2
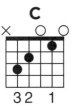	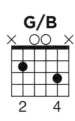	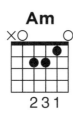	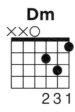	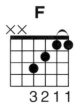	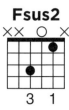

VERSE 1

Moderately

       C   G/B   Am   Dm   C   G/B
For all the times that you rained on my parade and all the clubs you get in using my name.

       C   G/B   Am   Dm   C
You think you broke my heart, oh, girl for goodness sake. You think I'm crying on my own.

    G/B   C   G/B   Am
Well, I ain't. And I didn't wanna write a song, 'cause I didn't want anyone thinking I still care.

Dm   C   G/B   C   G/B   Am
I don't, but you still hit my phone up. And, baby, I'll be moving on   and I think it should be

          Dm   C   G/B
something I don't wanna hold back. Maybe you should know that.

PRE-CHORUS

       Am   F   C   Am   F   C
My mama don't like you, and she likes everyone. And I never like to admit that I was wrong.

       Am   F   C   G
And I've been so caught up in my job, didn't see what's going on.

       Am F   G   N.C.
But now I know; I'm better sleeping on my own.

CHORUS

       C   G Am   F   C   Fsus2   C
'Cause if you like the way you look that much, oh baby you should go and love yourself.

       G Am   F   C   Fsus2   C
And if you think that I'm still holding on to something you should go and love yourself.

VERSE 2

```
        C              G/B       Am            Dm              C              G/B
But when you told me that you hated my friends, the only problem was with you and not them.

        C              G/B         Am            Dm            C              G/B
And every time you told me my opinion was wrong and tried to make me forget where I came from.

         C           G/B            Am
And I didn't wanna write a song,   'cause I didn't want anyone thinking I still care.

  Dm        C            G/B                 C     G/B           Am
I don't, but you still hit my phone up.  And, baby, I'll be moving on    and I think it should be something

       Dm         C            G/B
I don't wanna hold back.  Maybe you should know that.
```

REPEAT PRE-CHORUS

REPEAT CHORUS

INTERLUDE

For all the

VERSE 3

```
   C           G/B       Am         Dm           C          G/B
times that you made me feel small,  I fell in love, now I feel nothing at all.

     C           G/B       Am         Dm        C                 G/B
I never felt so low when I was vulnerable.  Was I a fool to let you break down my walls?
```

REPEAT CHORUS (2 TIMES)

Radioactive

Words and Music by Daniel Reynolds, Benjamin McKee,
Daniel Sermon, Alexander Grant and Josh Mosser

(Capo 2nd Fret)

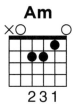 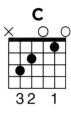 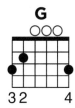 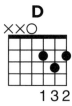 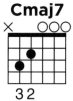

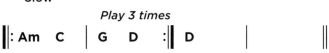

INTRO

Slow

Play 3 times

‖: Am C | G D :‖ D | | ‖

VERSE 1

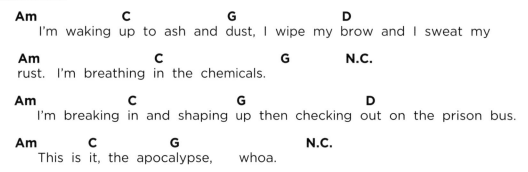

Am   C   G   D
    I'm waking up to ash and dust, I wipe my brow and I sweat my

Am   C   G   N.C.
rust. I'm breathing in the chemicals.

Am   C   G   D
    I'm breaking in and shaping up then checking out on the prison bus.

Am   C   G   N.C.
    This is it, the apocalypse,   whoa.

CHORUS

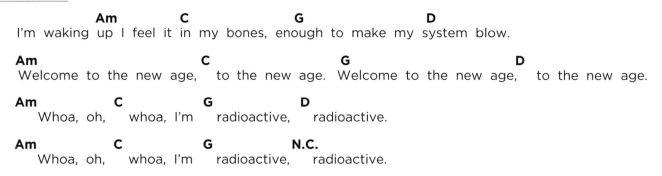

        Am   C   G   D
I'm waking up I feel it in my bones, enough to make my system blow.

Am   C   G   D
Welcome to the new age,   to the new age. Welcome to the new age,   to the new age.

Am   C   G   D
    Whoa, oh,   whoa, I'm radioactive, radioactive.

Am   C   G   N.C.
    Whoa, oh,   whoa, I'm radioactive, radioactive.

VERSE 2

```
    Am               C                  G                     D
        I raise my flag and dye my clothes.  It's a revolution

          Am                      C              G        D
    I suppose.  We're painted red to fit right in,     whoa.

    Am                 C              G                       D
        I'm breaking in and shaping up then checking out on the prison bus.

    Am          C          G                      N.C.
        This is it, the apocalypse,      whoa.
```

REPEAT CHORUS

BRIDGE

```
    Am             Cmaj7    G            D      Am          Cmaj7    G              D
    All systems go, the sun hasn't died.  Deep in my bones, straight from inside.
```

REPEAT CHORUS

Royals

Words and Music by Ella Yelich-O'Connor and Joel Little

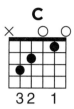
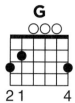

VERSE 1

Moderately slow

                N.C.(D)
I've never seen a diamond in the flesh. I cut my teeth on wedding rings in the movies.

And I'm not proud of my address in the torn up town, no post code envy.

PRE-CHORUS

                D
But every song's like gold teeth, Grey Goose, trippin' in the bathroom,

blood stains, ball gowns, trashin' the hotel room.
C   G
We don't care, we're drivin' Cadillacs in our dreams.

                D
But everybody's like: Cristal, Maybach, diamonds on your timepiece,

jet planes, islands, tigers on a gold leash.
C   G
We don't care, we aren't caught up in your love affair.

CHORUS

                D
And we'll never be royals. (Royals.) It don't run in our blood.

         C   G
That kind of lux just ain't for us. We crave a different kind of buzz.

         D
Let me be your ruler. (Ruler.) You can call me queen bee,

        C   G
and, baby, I'll rule. (I'll rule, I'll rule, I'll rule.)   Let me live that fantasy.

INTERLUDE

D | |

VERSE 2

N.C. (D)

My friends and I, we've cracked the code. We count our dollars on the train to the party.

And everyone who knows us knows that we're fine with this. We didn't come from money.

REPEAT PRE-CHORUS

REPEAT CHORUS

BRIDGE

N.C. (D)   **D C**

      Oh,   oh,   oh,   we're bigger than we ever dreamed,

G

  and I'm in love with being queen.

N.C. (D)   **D C**

      Oh,   oh,   oh,   life is great without a care.

       G

We aren't caught up in your love affair.

REPEAT CHORUS

Say Something

Words and Music by Ian Axel, Chad Vaccarino and Mike Campbell

(Capo 2nd Fret)

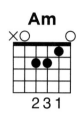 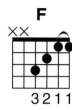 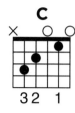 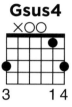 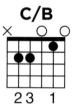

INTRO

Moderately fast

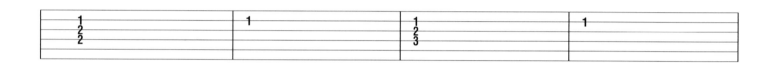

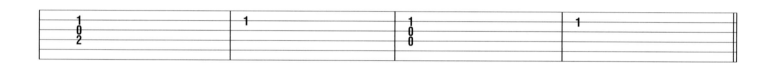

CHORUS 1

Am	F	C	Gsus4

Say something, I'm giving up on you.

Am	F	C	Gsus4

I'll be the one if you want me to.

Am	F	C	Gsus4

Anywhere I would have followed you.

Am	F	C	Gsus4

Say something, I'm giving up on you.

VERSE 1

C	C/B	F	C	Gsus4

And I am feeling so small. It was over my head; I know nothing at all.

VERSE 2

```
     C                C/B        F                                    C          Gsus4
And I will stumble and fall.  I'm still learning to love, just starting to crawl.
```

CHORUS 2

```
Am                 F                  C          Gsus4
   Say something, I'm giving up on you.

Am                 F                  C          Gsus4
   I'm sorry that I couldn't get to you.

Am             F                      C          Gsus4
   Anywhere I would have followed you.

Am                 F                  C          Gsus4
   Say something, I'm giving up on you.
```

VERSE 3

```
     C                C/B        F                                 C         Gsus4
And I will swallow my pride.  You're the one that I love, and I'm saying goodbye.
```

CHORUS 3

```
Am                 F              C          Gsus4
   Say something, I'm giving up on you.

Am                 F              C          Gsus4
   And I'm sorry that I couldn't get to you.

Am             F                  C          Gsus4
   And anywhere I would have followed you.

Am                 F              C          Gsus4
   Say something, I'm giving up on you.

Am                 F              C          Gsus4
   Say something, I'm giving up on you.

Am                 F        C
   Say something.
                         •
```

Shallow

from A STAR IS BORN

Words and Music by Stefani Germanotta, Mark Ronson,
Andrew Wyatt and Anthony Rossomando

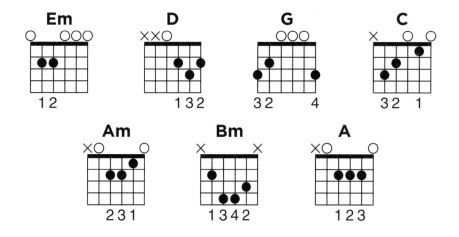

INTRO

Moderately slow

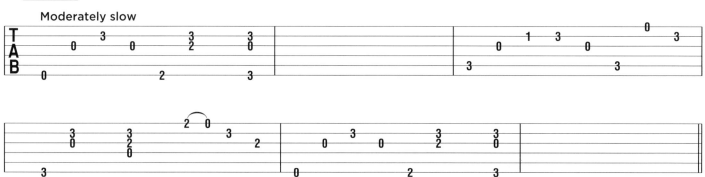

VERSE 1

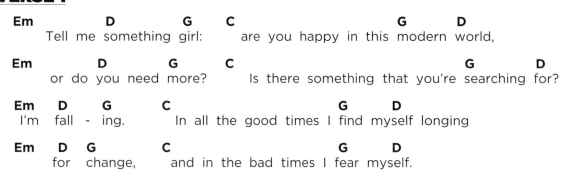

Em   D   G   C   G   D
Tell me something girl: are you happy in this modern world,

Em   D   G   C   G   D
or do you need more?   Is there something that you're searching for?

Em   D   G   C   G   D
I'm fall - ing.   In all the good times I find myself longing

Em   D G   C   G   D
for change,   and in the bad times I fear myself.

INTERLUDE

```
     3     3  3                        3     3  3
  0    0  2    0                     0    0  2    0
  0        2     3                   0        2     3
```

VERSE 2

Em   D   G C   G   D
Tell me something boy: aren't you tired try'n' to fill that void,

Em   D   G   C   G   D
or do you need more? Ain't it hard keeping it so hardcore?

Em D G   C   G   D
I'm fall - ing. In all the good times I find myself longing

Em D G   C   G   D
for change, and in the bad times I fear myself.

CHORUS

Am   D   G   D Em
I'm off the deep end. Watch as I dive in. I'll never meet the ground.

Am   D   G   D Em
Crash through the surface, where they can't hurt us. We're far from the shallow now.

Am   D   G   D   Em
In the shal, - al shal, - al - low, in the shal, shal, - al, - al, - al, - low.

Am   D   G   D   Em
In the shal, - al shal, - al - low, we're far from the shal - low now.

BRIDGE

Bm   D A   Em   Bm   D   A
oh, ah,   ah, ah,   oh, ah, ah.

REPEAT CHORUS

Someone Like You

Words and Music by Adele Adkins and Dan Wilson

(Capo 2nd Fret)

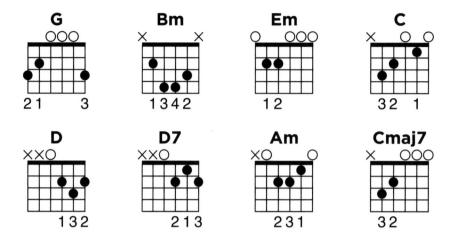

INTRO

VERSE 1

| G | | Bm | | Em | | C |
heard that you're settled down, that you found a girl and you're married now.

| G | | Bm | | Em | | C |
I heard that your dreams came true, guess she gave you things I didn't give to you.

| G | | Bm | | Em | | C |
Old friend, why are you so shy? Ain't like you to hold back or hide from the light.

PRE-CHORUS 1

| D | | Em | | C |
I hate to turn up out of the blue uninvited, but I couldn't stay away, I couldn't fight it.

| D | | Em | | C | D7 | C |
I had hoped you'd see my face and that you'd be reminded that for me it isn't over.

CHORUS 1

```
 G                    D            Em          C                    G            D         Em    C
    Nevermind, I'll find someone like   you.        I wish nothing but the best for you    two.

       G        D        Em          C
Don't forget me, I beg.  I remember  you  said,

            G                 D                      Em          C
"Sometime it lasts in love, but sometimes it hurts instead."

            G                 D                      Em          C
Sometimes it lasts in love, but sometimes it hurts instead.
```

VERSE 2

```
 G                Bm              Em                      C
    You know how the   time flies, only   yesterday was the time of our lives.

       G              Bm                  Em                   C
We were born and raised in a   summer haze, bound by the surprise of our glory days.
```

PRE-CHORUS 2

```
      D                          Em                 C
I hate to turn up out of the blue uninvited, but I couldn't stay away, I couldn't fight it.

       D                            Em                        C        D7      C D7
I had hoped you'd see my face and that you'd be reminded that for me it isn't over.
```

CHORUS 2

```
 G                    D            Em    C       G            D         Em  C
    Nevermind, I'll find someone like   you.     I wish nothing but the best for you   two.

       G      D     Em          C
Don't forget me, I beg.  I remember you said,

            G                 D                      Em          C
"Sometime it lasts in love, but sometimes it hurts instead."
```

BRIDGE

```
 D                                    Em
Nothing compares, no worries or cares, regrets and mistakes, they're memories made.

 C                                 Am      G        C    D7
Who would have known how bittersweet this would taste?
```

REPEAT CHORUS 2

REPEAT CHORUS 1

OUTRO

```
 C            | D7   Cmaj7  | C          | G          ‖
```

Stay with Me

Words and Music by Sam Smith, James Napier,
William Edward Phillips, Tom Petty and Jeff Lynne

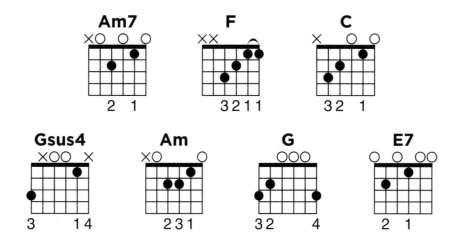

Moderately fast

‖: Am7   F   C | :‖

VERSE 1

Am7   **F**   **C**
Guess it's true, I'm not good at a one night stand.

Am7   **F**   **C**
I still need love 'cause I'm just a man.

Am7   **F**   **C**
These nights never seem to go to plan.

Am7   **Gsus4**   **C**
I don't want you to leave, will you hold my hand?   Oh, won't you

CHORUS 1

Am   **F**   **C**   **Am** **F**   **C**   **G**
stay   with   me?   'Cause you're   all   I   need.   This ain't

Am   **F**   **C**   **E7**   **Am**   **F**   **C**
love, it's clear to see.   But darling,   stay   with   me.

VERSE 2

Am7   F   C
Why am I so emotional?

Am7   F   C
No, it's not a good look. Gain some self-control.

Am7   F   C
And deep down I know this never works.

Am7   Gsus4   C
But you can lay with me so it doesn't hurt.   Oh, won't you

REPEAT CHORUS

BRIDGE

      Am   F   C   Am   F   C
Oh,   oh.

      Am   F   C   Am   F   C
Oh,   oh.   Oh, won't you

CHORUS 2

Am   F   C   Am   F   C   G
   stay   with   me?   'Cause you're   all   I   need.   This ain't

Am   F   C   E7   Am   F   C
   love, it's clear to see.   But darling,   stay   with   me.   Oh, won't you

REPEAT CHORUS 1

Tennessee Whiskey

Words and Music by Dean Dillon and Linda Hargrove

(Capo 2nd Fret)

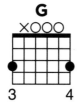
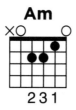
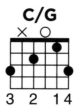

INTRO

Slow

G | |Am | |

    | |G   C/G| G ||

VERSE 1

G
    Used to spend my nights out in the barrooms,   Am

                                         G C/G G
liquor was the only love I'd known.

                                            Am
    But you rescued me from reaching for the bottom

                                        G C/G G
and brought me back from being too far gone.

CHORUS

              G   Am
You're as smooth as Tennessee whiskey.

                              G C/G G
You're as sweet as strawberry wine.

                                Am
You're as warm as a glass of brandy.

                                     G C/G G
And, honey, I stay stoned on your love all the time.

VERSE 2

G   Am
I've looked for love in all the same old places,

                               G C/G G
found the bottom of the bottle's always dry.

                                         Am
But when you poured out your heart I didn't waste it

                                   G C/G G
'cause there's nothing like your love to get me high.

REPEAT CHORUS (3 TIMES)

Second time, guitar solo

OUTRO-CHORUS

              G   Am
You're as smooth as Tennessee whiskey,

                           G   C/G   G
Tennessee whiskey, Tennessee whiskey.

                                Am
You're as smooth as Tennessee whiskey,

                           G
Tennessee whiskey, Tennessee whiskey.

Thinking Out Loud

Words and Music by Ed Sheeran and Amy Wadge

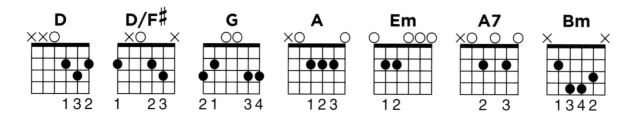

VERSE 1

Moderately slow

D   D/F#   G   A
When your legs don't work like they used to before

D   D/F#   G   A
and I can't sweep you off of your feet,

D   D/F#   G   A
will your mouth still remember the taste of my love?

D   D/F#   G   A
Will your eyes still smile from your cheeks?

VERSE 2

          D   D/F#   G   A
And darling, I   will be loving you   till we're seventy.

D   D/F#   G   A

         D   D/F#   G   A
And baby, my   heart could still fall as   hard at twenty-three.

D   D/F#   G   A
                         And I'm thinkin' 'bout how

PRE-CHORUS 1

Em   A7   D   Em   A7
people fall in love in mysterious ways, maybe just the touch of a hand.

     Em   A7   Bm   Em   A7
Well me, I fall in love with you ev'ry single day. And I just wanna tell you I am.

N.C.
So honey, now

CHORUS 1

D   D/F♯   G   A
take me into your loving arms.

D   D/F♯   G   A
Kiss me under the light of a

D   D/F♯   G   A
thousand stars.   Place your head on my beating heart.

D   D/F♯   G A   Bm A   G D/F♯ Em   A   D
I'm thinking out loud   maybe we found love right where we are.

VERSE 3

D   D/F♯   G   A
When my hair's all but gone and my memory fades

D   D/F♯   G   A
and the crowds don't remember my name,

D   D/F♯   G   A
when my hands   don't play the strings the same way,   mm,

D   D/F♯   G   A
mm,   I know you will still love me the same.

VERSE 4

            D   D/F♯   G   A
'Cause honey, your   soul could never grow   old, its evergreen.

D   D/F♯   G   A

            D   D/F♯   G   A
And baby, your   smile's forever in   my mind and memory.

D   D/F♯   G   A
I'm thinkin' 'bout how

PRE-CHORUS 2

Em   A7   D   Em   A7
people fall in love in mysterious ways, and maybe it's all part of a plan.

    Em   A7 Bm   Em   A7
Well, I'll just keep on making the same   mistakes   hoping that you'll understand

N.C.
that baby, now,

REPEAT CHORUS 1

OUTRO

     Bm A   G D/F♯ Em   A   D
Baby, we found love right where we are.

     Bm A   G D/F♯ Em   A   D
And, we found love right where we are.

This Is Me
from THE GREATEST SHOWMAN
Words and Music by Benj Pasek and Justin Paul

(Capo 2nd Fret)

Am    G 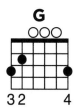   C 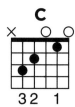   F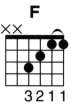

INTRO

Moderately

‖: Am | G | C | :‖

VERSE 1

```
Am                  G          C
 I am not a stranger   to the dark.

         F      Am           G
Hide away,   they say, 'cause we don't want your broken parts.

     Am              G   C
I've learned to be ashamed of all     my scars.

         F      Am          G
Run away,   they say, no one'll love you as you are. But
```

PRE-CHORUS

```
 F                           G        Am
  I won't let them break me down to dust.

                  G     C          G
I know that there's a place for us,   for we are glorious.
```

CHORUS 1

        C
When the sharpest words wanna cut me down,

        Am
I'm gonna send a flood, gonna drown 'em out.

        F   G   N.C.
I am brave, I am bruised. I am who I'm meant to be. This is me.

C
      Look out, 'cause here I come,

        Am
     and I'm marchin' on to the beat I drum.

        F   G   N.C.
I'm not scared to be seen; I make no apologies. This is me.

INTERLUDE

C   Am   F   G   N.C.
Oh. Oh.   Oh. Oh. Oh.   Oh. Oh.   Oh, oh.

VERSE 2

     Am   G   C
Another round of bullets hits my skin.

           F   Am   G
Well, fire away,   'cause today I won't let the shame sink in.

      Am   G   C
We are burstin' through the barricades and reachin' for the sun.

      F   Am   G
(We are warriors.)   Yeah, that's what we've become.

BRIDGE

      C   Am
And I know that I deserve your love.

                     F   G
There's nothing I'm not worthy of.

REPEAT CHORUS 1

OUTRO

     C
Whenever the words wanna cut me down,

                     Am
I'll send a flood to drown them out.

     F   G   N.C.(C)
Oh.   Oh. Oh.   Oh, oh. This is me.

A Thousand Years
from the Summit Entertainment film
THE TWILIGHT SAGA: BREAKING DAWN - PART 1

Words and Music by David Hodges and Christina Perri

(Capo 3rd Fret)

G   D   Em   C   Am

INTRO

Moderately slow

| G | | D | Em | | | D | |
| C | | | G | | D | | |

VERSE 1

C   G
Heart beats fast, colors and promises.

           Em   D   G C
How to be brave? How can I love when I'm afraid to fall?

                     G   Em   D G   Am
But watching you stand alone, all of my doubt suddenly goes away somehow.

        Em   D
One step clos - er.

CHORUS 1

G   D
I have died ev'ry day waiting for you.

Em   D   C
Darling, don't be afraid, I have loved you for a thousand years;

                       G   D
I'll love you for a thousand more.

INTERLUDE 1

| C | | |

VERSE 2

C   G
Time stands still, beauty in all she is.

    Em   D G C   G
I will be brave, I will not let anything take away what's standing in front of me.

    Em   D   G   Am
Every breath, every hour has come to this.

    D Em D
One step clos - er.

REPEAT CHORUS 1

CHORUS 2

    G   D
And all along I believed I would find you.

Em   D   C
Time has brought your heart to me, I have loved you for a thousand years;

      G   D
I'll love you for a thousand more.

INTERLUDE 2

G | D |Em | D |

C | |G | ‖

BRIDGE

Am   Em D
  One step clos - er.

Am   D Em D
  One step clos - er.

REPEAT CHORUS 1

REPEAT CHORUS 2

OUTRO

C | |G | |

C | |Em |D |C   ‖

When I Was Your Man

Words and Music by Bruno Mars, Ari Levine, Philip Lawrence and Andrew Wyatt

(Capo 5th Fret)

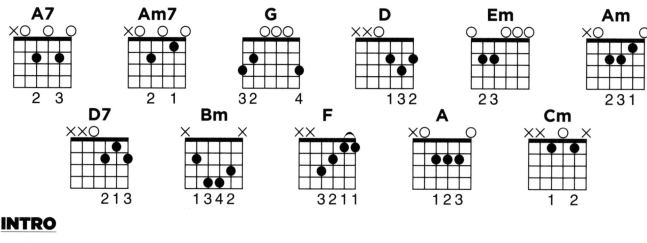

INTRO

Slow

| A7 | Am7 | G | | A7 | Am7 | G | D ||

VERSE 1

Em   **G**   **Am**
Same bed, but it feels just a little bit bigger now.

D   **D7**   **G**   **Bm**
Our song on the radio, but it don't sound the same.

Em   **G**   **Am**
When our friends talk about you, all it does is just tear me down,

D   **G**   **Bm**
'cause my heart breaks a little when I hear   your name. It all sounds like,

PRE-CHORUS

Em   **Bm**   **F**   **G**   **D N.C.**
"Oo, hoo."   Mm, too young, too dumb to realize   that I should've bought you

CHORUS 1

C   **D**   **G**
flowers   and held your hand; should've gave you all my

C   **D**   **G**
hours   when I had the chance; take you to ev'ry

C   **D**   **Em** **A**
party, 'cause all you wanted to do was dance. Now my baby's

C   **Cm**   **G**   **C G** **D**
dancing, but she's dancing with another man.

VERSE 2

```
Em              G                   Am
    My pride, my ego, my needs and my selfish ways

D                       D7                G         Bm
    caused a good, strong woman like you to walk out my life.

            Em    G                   Am
Now I'll never,    never get to clean up the mess I've made, oh,

D                                   G         Bm
    and it haunts me ev'ry time I close    my eyes. It all just sounds like,
```

REPEAT PRE-CHORUS

CHORUS 2

```
C         D           G
flowers        and held your hand; should've gave you all my

C         D               G
hours        when I had the chance; take you to ev'ry

C                   D           Em    A
party, 'cause all you wanted to do was dance.  Now my baby's

C              Cm              G
dancing, but she's dancing with another man.
```

BRIDGE

```
            C           D               G         D  Em      Bm
    Although it hurts, I'll be the first to say that I was wrong.

        A                                   Am
Oh I know I'm prob'ly much too late to try and apologize for my mistakes.

            D           N.C.
But I just want you to know,      I hope he buys you
```

OUTRO-CHORUS

```
C         D               G
flowers;     I hope he holds your hand; give you all his

C         D           G
hours        when he has the chance; take you to ev'ry

C             D                   Em   A
party, 'cause I remember how much you love to dance; do all the things I

C               Cm          G    A
    should've done     when I was your man. Do all the things I

C               Cm          G
    should've done,    when I was your man.
```

EASY GUITAR WITH NOTES & TAB

This series features simplified arrangements with notes, tab, chord charts, and strum and pick patterns.

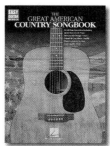  

MIXED FOLIOS

00702287 Acoustic	$19.99	
00702002 Acoustic Rock Hits for Easy Guitar	$17.99	
00702166 All-Time Best Guitar Collection	$29.99	
00702232 Best Acoustic Songs for Easy Guitar	$16.99	
00119835 Best Children's Songs	$16.99	
00703055 The Big Book of Nursery Rhymes & Children's Songs	$16.99	
00698978 Big Christmas Collection	$19.99	
00702394 Bluegrass Songs for Easy Guitar	$15.99	
00289632 Bohemian Rhapsody	$19.99	
00703387 Celtic Classics	$16.99	
00224808 Chart Hits of 2016-2017	$14.99	
00267383 Chart Hits of 2017-2018	$14.99	
00334293 Chart Hits of 2019-2020	$16.99	
00403479 Chart Hits of 2021-2022	$16.99	
00702149 Children's Christian Songbook	$9.99	
00702028 Christmas Classics	$9.99	
00101779 Christmas Guitar	$16.99	
00702141 Classic Rock	$8.95	
00159642 Classical Melodies	$12.99	
00253933 Disney/Pixar's Coco	$19.99	
00702203 CMT's 100 Greatest Country Songs	$34.99	
00702283 The Contemporary Christian Collection	$16.99	

00196954 Contemporary Disney	$19.99	
00702239 Country Classics for Easy Guitar	$24.99	
00702257 Easy Acoustic Guitar Songs	$17.99	
00702041 Favorite Hymns for Easy Guitar	$12.99	
00222701 Folk Pop Songs	$19.99	
00126894 Frozen	$14.99	
00333922 Frozen 2	$14.99	
00702286 Glee	$16.99	
00702160 The Great American Country Songbook	$19.99	
00702148 Great American Gospel for Guitar	$14.99	
00702050 Great Classical Themes for Easy Guitar	$9.99	
00148030 Halloween Guitar Songs	$17.99	
00702273 Irish Songs	$14.99	
00192503 Jazz Classics for Easy Guitar	$16.99	
00702275 Jazz Favorites for Easy Guitar	$17.99	
00702274 Jazz Standards for Easy Guitar	$19.99	
00702162 Jumbo Easy Guitar Songbook	$24.99	
00232285 La La Land	$16.99	
00702258 Legends of Rock	$14.99	
00702189 MTV's 100 Greatest Pop Songs	$34.99	
00702272 1950s Rock	$16.99	
00702271 1960s Rock	$16.99	
00702270 1970s Rock	$24.99	
00702269 1980s Rock	$16.99	

00702268 1990s Rock	$24.99	
00369043 Rock Songs for Kids	$14.99	
00109725 Once	$14.99	
00702187 Selections from O Brother Where Art Thou?	$19.99	
00702178 100 Songs for Kids	$16.99	
00702515 Pirates of the Caribbean	$17.99	
00702125 Praise and Worship for Guitar	$14.99	
00287930 Songs from *A Star Is Born, The Greatest Showman, La La Land*, and More Movie Musicals	$16.99	
00702285 Southern Rock Hits	$12.99	
00156420 Star Wars Music	$16.99	
00121535 30 Easy Celtic Guitar Solos	$16.99	
00244654 Top Hits of 2017	$14.99	
00283786 Top Hits of 2018	$14.99	
00302269 Top Hits of 2019	$14.99	
00355779 Top Hits of 2020	$14.99	
00374083 Top Hits of 2021	$16.99	
00702294 Top Worship Hits	$17.99	
00702255 VH1's 100 Greatest Hard Rock Songs	$39.99	
00702175 VH1's 100 Greatest Songs of Rock and Roll	$34.99	
00702253 Wicked	$12.99	

ARTIST COLLECTIONS

00702267 AC/DC for Easy Guitar	$17.99	
00156221 Adele – 25	$16.99	
00396889 Adele – 30	$19.99	
00702040 Best of the Allman Brothers	$16.99	
00702865 J.S. Bach for Easy Guitar	$15.99	
00702169 Best of The Beach Boys	$16.99	
00702292 The Beatles — 1	$22.99	
00125796 Best of Chuck Berry	$16.99	
00702201 The Essential Black Sabbath	$15.99	
00702250 blink-182 — Greatest Hits	$19.99	
02501615 Zac Brown Band — The Foundation	$19.99	
02501621 Zac Brown Band — You Get What You Give	$16.99	
00702043 Best of Johnny Cash	$19.99	
00702090 Eric Clapton's Best	$16.99	
00702086 Eric Clapton — from the Album Unplugged	$17.99	
00702202 The Essential Eric Clapton	$19.99	
00702053 Best of Patsy Cline	$17.99	
00222697 Very Best of Coldplay – 2nd Edition	$17.99	
00702229 The Very Best of Creedence Clearwater Revival	$16.99	
00702145 Best of Jim Croce	$16.99	
00702278 Crosby, Stills & Nash	$12.99	
14042809 Bob Dylan	$15.99	
00702276 Fleetwood Mac — Easy Guitar Collection	$17.99	
00139462 The Very Best of Grateful Dead	$17.99	
00702136 Best of Merle Haggard	$19.99	
00702227 Jimi Hendrix — Smash Hits	$19.99	
00702288 Best of Hillsong United	$12.99	
00702236 Best of Antonio Carlos Jobim	$15.99	

00702245 Elton John — Greatest Hits 1970–2002	$19.99	
00129855 Jack Johnson	$17.99	
00702204 Robert Johnson	$16.99	
00702234 Selections from Toby Keith — 35 Biggest Hits	$12.95	
00702003 Kiss	$16.99	
00702216 Lynyrd Skynyrd	$17.99	
00702182 The Essential Bob Marley	$17.99	
00146081 Maroon 5	$14.99	
00121925 Bruno Mars – Unorthodox Jukebox	$12.99	
00702248 Paul McCartney — All the Best	$14.99	
00125484 The Best of MercyMe	$12.99	
00702209 Steve Miller Band — Young Hearts (Greatest Hits)	$12.95	
00124167 Jason Mraz	$15.99	
00702096 Best of Nirvana	$17.99	
00702211 The Offspring — Greatest Hits	$17.99	
00138026 One Direction	$17.99	
00702030 Best of Roy Orbison	$17.99	
00702144 Best of Ozzy Osbourne	$14.99	
00702279 Tom Petty	$17.99	
00102911 Pink Floyd	$17.99	
00702139 Elvis Country Favorites	$19.99	
00702293 The Very Best of Prince	$22.99	
00699415 Best of Queen for Guitar	$16.99	
00109279 Best of R.E.M.	$14.99	
00702208 Red Hot Chili Peppers — Greatest Hits	$19.99	
00198960 The Rolling Stones	$17.99	
00174793 The Very Best of Santana	$16.99	
00702196 Best of Bob Seger	$16.99	
00146046 Ed Sheeran	$19.99	

00702252 Frank Sinatra — Nothing But the Best	$12.99	
00702010 Best of Rod Stewart	$17.99	
00702049 Best of George Strait	$17.99	
00702259 Taylor Swift for Easy Guitar	$15.99	
00359800 Taylor Swift – Easy Guitar Anthology	$24.99	
00702260 Taylor Swift — Fearless	$14.99	
00139727 Taylor Swift — 1989	$19.99	
00115960 Taylor Swift — Red	$16.99	
00253667 Taylor Swift — Reputation	$17.99	
00702290 Taylor Swift — Speak Now	$16.99	
00232849 Chris Tomlin Collection – 2nd Edition	$14.99	
00702226 Chris Tomlin — See the Morning	$12.95	
00148643 Train	$14.99	
00702427 U2 — 18 Singles	$19.99	
00702108 Best of Stevie Ray Vaughan	$17.99	
00279005 The Who	$14.99	
00702123 Best of Hank Williams	$15.99	
00194548 Best of John Williams	$14.99	
00702228 Neil Young — Greatest Hits	$17.99	
00119133 Neil Young — Harvest	$16.99	

Prices, contents and availability subject to change without notice.